# Millom

## in old picture postcards volume 2

by
Bill Myers

European Library – Zaltbommel/Netherlands

ISBN10: 90 288 5842 3
ISBN13: 978 90 288 5842 8

© 1994  European Library – Zaltbommel/Netherlands
© 2010  Reprint of the original edition of 1994

European Library
post office box 49
NL – 5300 AA  Zaltbommel/The Netherlands
telephone: 0031 418 513144
fax: 0031 418 515515
e-mail:publisher@eurobib.nl

# INTRODUCTION

A century ago Millom was entering the last phase of a building boom which had turned open fields on the West Cumberland coastline into a new town in little more than thirty years.

In 1894 Millom saw the completion of a number of buildings which are now familiar parts of the modern town. They include Millom Conservative Club in Lapstone Road, Millom Police Station and court house, part of Duke Street and the former post office building on the corner of Wellington Street and Katherine Street. Another building to celebrate a centenary in 1994 is the Bible Christian Sunday School in Newton Street, which has more recently been an employment exchange and leather goods factory.

To meet this demand for new houses and public buildings there was a wide range of local builders and contractors. They were led by William Bradley of Salthouse Road, who manufactured most of Millom's bricks and tiles as well as being a builder, joiner, contractor, painter and decorator. At that time Millom and Haverigg had fifteen other firms engaged in various aspects of the building trade. By around 1905 those firms had completed the construction of Millom and there was relatively little further change until local authority housing and new private estates began to expand the town again after the First World War.

1894 was also a big year for industrial relations at Millom's Hodbarrow Mines with the directors deciding to stay neutral on the issue of trade union membership for miners. The company would do nothing to obstruct membership, but issued notices preventing any union recruiting on company land or in company time. One 1894 notice read: 'The progress of work is being seriously interfered with by members of the union who take up the time of other miners by canvassing in other workings than their own.'

Millom in 1894 was a prosperous place. In 1871 the value placed on land in Millom for local government rates was just £14,000, but by 1881 house building and rapid growth at Hodbarrow Mines and Millom Ironworks pushed that figure to £84,000. By 1901 the value had risen still further to £107,093. From 1892 to 1894 production of iron ore at Hodbarrow reached record levels with over 500,000 tons raised each year. A total of £100,000 per year was being paid in dividends to thankful shareholders.

By 1901 Millom Ironworks had six furnaces in production and was described as: 'Of the most modern character and are replete with every recent invention for the economical production of pig iron.' That new technology included the installation in 1898 of a Uehling type pig casting machine, which was the first of its kind in Great Britain.

With prosperity came ever greater numbers of people seeking work. In 1861 the Millom parish, including Thwaites and Ulpha, had fewer than 1,000 people, yet by 1871 Millom alone had 4,307. In the 1881 census it was 7,698 and by 1901 had risen to 10,426, in part due to a massive influx of labourers working on the Hodbarrow Outer Barrier or Sea Wall.

Hodbarrow alone provided work for 1,350 people in 1901

with the ironworks employing several hundred more.

To administer this growing town the old Local Board was transformed by the 1894 Local Government Act into an urban district council with 16 members. In 1894 Millom also had two home-grown newspapers. The Millom Weekly Gazette was published on Fridays by Richard Sprague of Lapstone Road, while the Millom News was issued on Tuesdays and Saturdays by Market Square printer William Atkinson. Millom had twenty public houses and beer sellers to help quench the thirst of miners and foundry workers. Many of those traditional pubs have fallen victim to re-development schemes or have been converted into private homes. They include the Ironworks public house in Duddon Street, The Royal in Queen Street, the Bottom Ship in Albert Street and The Crown in Lord Street.

Religion played a major part in the life of the town and in 1894 Millom and Haverigg had at least thirteen churches and chapels. Among those to fold in the past century are the Primitive Methodists at Holborn Hill and Haverigg, the Welsh Calvanistic Methodists and the Bible Christians in Newton Street.

A century ago Millom supported a vast range of specialised shops and trades, many of which have long since vanished. The town had no fewer than thirteen butchers, fifteen shoe shops, eleven greengrocers and ten confectioners. If you needed a new outfit the town had thirteen milliners or dressmakers and four tailors. If times were hard there were pawnbrokers in both King Street and Queen Street, or you could see the manager at Millom branches of the Liverpool, Cumberland Union Bank or Lancaster Bank.

There were also shops in streets where today there are only houses, or where the whole street has been swept away by the modern age. In 1894 John Steele was a grocer and George Seaman a shopkeeper in the long since demolished Borwick Rails, near Millom Ironworks. Surrey Street had a grocer and two dressmakers, Lord Street had a butcher's shop and Albert Street had five shopkeepers, a lodging house, two dressmakers, a clogger and a branch of the Co-Operative Society.

This second volume of pictures showing Millom and its surrounding villages marks another important development in 1894, the first British picture postcards. The vast majority of historic views which survive of Millom's shops, streets and industries are on postcards. They were produced by big national firms but more often by local photographers, chemist shops or stationers to sell at a penny each to summer visitors, or to go into the family albums of Millom's Victorian and Edwardian postcard collectors.

The British Post Office authorised the first privately produced picture postcards on 1st September in 1894 and opened the floodgates to a new industry churning out millions of cards a year. Those postcards are still avidly saved today and the pictures in this volume are a selection from a private archive of more than 10,000 Cumbrian cards belonging to Millom collector Bill Myers.

RECEPTION OF MT FULLERTON M.P. JAN 26TH 1906

1. *Meeting the new M.P.* Millom people get to meet their new Member of Parliament in this postcard view of Newton Street in 1906. The event was captured on film on 26th January, just a few days after Liberal candidate Mr. H. Fullerton won the Egremont Division, which then included Millom, in the General Election. His successful election campaign came despite controversy sparked by local press reports claiming use of a false letter to urge all Millom's Roman Catholics to vote Liberal. In the days before television and radio broadcasts a political speech, or a visit by a politician, could draw huge crowds. Shown in the background of this public reception is Thompson's butchers and a number of Newton Street shops facing the junction with Queen Street.

MARKET SQUARE. MILLOM

2. *Town Hall Clock, Millom.* Millom Town Hall clock is one of the enduring features which make the town what it is, but it was almost never built. In 1878 a stormy government inquiry was held in the Magistrates Court at Millom Public Hall to decide on a controversial extraordinary loan sought by Millom Local Board. The board wanted £10,500 for gas and water works and £3,500 for a market house and offices in the Market Square, but was opposed by 98 ratepayers and property owners. Mr. Atter, for the objectors, said the board was acting against property owners and was reckless in spending money. Thanks to Local Government Board inspector Col Ponsonby Cox the town hall was built and can be seen on this postcard of 1910.

3. *Window shopping in Millom.* This postcard shows a typical Edwardian small shop in Millom. The staff of five pose for the photographer around 1905 outside the 'Hippo' Dining Rooms. The window includes examples of the food available, a lengthy menu and advertisements for what appear to be early moving picture shows visiting Millom. Research in old trade directories has so far failed to identify which street the picture was taken in, but Holborn Hill and St. George's Terrace are strong possibilities. A good number of Millom's shops still retain similar ornate wooden shop window frames and doorways but many more have been replaced by modern alternatives.

LAPSTONE ROAD AND WELLINGTON STREET, MILLOM.

4. *Ward the stationer, Millom.* This postcard shows the heart of Millom's shopping centre, where Wellington Street meets Crown Street and Lapstone Road. The main building in the centre is now a clothing shop but at the turn of the century was the stationery business of Charles Ward. Indeed this postcard was produced for, and sold in large quantities by, Ward's from the First World War until the late 1920s. This example was posted in 1926. There are racks of postcards on the outside wall and the window is filled with Ward's products and promotional posters for steam ship passages to the United States of America and Canada with White Star Shipping Line. Ward's is faced by the Millom Co-Operative headquarters and the sign on the left-hand edge of the postcard for luncheons and teas is the Temperance Hotel and confectioner's business of Harry Deacon in Lapstone Road.

5. *Lapstone Road, Millom*. This elegant Edwardian lady is shown outside a house in Lapstone Road, Millom. The picture was taken in 1903 and shows part of the block of Victorian homes facing the Lapstone House residential home and the Millom letter and parcel sorting office. It features the wife of William John Yarr, a leading Millom industrialist with a brass and iron foundry in Millom Road. She was writing to Jonty Yarr, probably her son, who was a pupil at the Royal Masonic School at Bushey, Hertfordshire. Many Millom homes and public buildings had elaborate cast iron railings similar to those in Lapstone Road, but most were cut up for scrap during the Second World War.

Wellington Street, Millom

*an antique view before Will took Wellington St shop*

6. *Wellington Street, Millom.* This postcard dated 1903 shows the top end of Wellington Street, just below Millom Co-Operative Society, which is now Millom Builders' Merchants. The two shops on the right-hand edge, with pointed roofs, are now part of the Fashion House and Scurrah's Newsagents. In 1894 they were the shops of Mrs. Hannah Birkett and Richard Kitchen, the tobacconist. By 1906 the businesses were in the hands of Ellen Gendle, a milliner, and clockmaker Anthony Shackley, who was still trading until at least 1934. The shop on the right-hand edge, with a clock above the door, is believed to be W. Hall, the jeweller, with Flynn's grocery shop next door. Both shops are now a baby clothing stockist.

7. *Wellington Street, Millom.* This 1906 view shows a horse and cart making deliveries to shops in Wellington Street, Millom. On the left is the cobbled back alley to Nelson Street and a garage, which has been demolished and is now a solid fuel agency. Next to it was the department store of John Floyd which sold groceries, hardware and provisions. Today the building is the Cellar Five off-licence and the Waterloo House Surgery. Behind the gas lamp on the right can be made out the shop sign of Roberts, which is now the Swinton Insurance Agency. This postcard was produced by the Milton Company of London but was sold by W.J. Warnock, the stationer of 68 Wellington Street, Millom.

8. *Edwardian fire damage.* This postcard from 29th August 1910 shows Number 50 Wellington Street, Millom. At that time the building was owned by John Floyd, a grocer, provision and hardware dealer. The picture shows the gable end of the building in a state of dereliction, with its windows and doors broken, and its roof open to the weather. A ladder tied to the wall and what looks like a hose pipe would seem to indicate that the damage was the result of a serious fire. The building is now part of the Cellar Five Off-Licence and has seen considerable change, but the outline of the gable end windows and goods doorways can still be seen.

9. *Lapstone Road Parade.* Everything came to a halt for the annual summer parade day. On this postcard of around 1910 crowds can be seen lining both sides of Wellington Street and they have blocked off Lapstone Road outside the Conservative Club. The carnival queen can just be seen behind the coach driver in this top hat. On the left is Deacon's Commercial Hotel which is now a hot food takeaway with flats above. The big sandstone and slate shop facing into Lapstone Road is now a clothing store, but in 1910 was Ward's the printer and stationer. Window displays include an invitation to a lecture on Canada, as Ward's was an emigration agent.

10. *Crowning the Queen, 1917*. Millom has a long tradition of processions and carnival parades stretching from the Victorian era to the present day. This postcard dated 16th June 1917 shows the crowning ceremony for a Millom Carnival Queen, probably on farmland at Devonshire Road. The Barrow News of 11th June 1881 reported on the annual procession of the friendly societies held through the streets of Millom on Whitsuntide Tuesday. It involved the Rising Star Lodge of the Free and Independent Order of Mechanics and the Millom Castle Lodge of the Independent Order of Mechanics. Music along the parade route was provided by Haverigg Brass Band, Holborn Hill Royal Brass Band and St. George's Drum and Fife Band. The Millom Castle Lodge of Mechanics had been founded in April 1874 and met at the Queen's Hotel, then run by Mr. Kitchen.

11. *Moor Terrace, Millom.* The decorations were hung out in June 1927 for the visit to Millom of the Prince of Wales. This picture shows strings of coloured bunting draped across the houses in Moor Terrace, Millom. Prince Edward came to the town on 29th June as part of a West Cumbrian tour, which included Egremont. Around the same time Millom also had a visit by the Duke of Kent, who is thought to have toured the Millom Social Centre in Lonsdale Road to see a number of local boxers in action. The latest royal visit to Millom was in November 1959 by Princess Alexandra for the official opening of Millom School. School authorities named the main assembly room as The Alexandra Hall to mark the visit.

Millom & Black Combe

12. *Station Hotel, Millom.* The photographer who took this Edwardian view of Millom chose a high vantage point to see over the backyards and roof tops to look towards Millom Railway Station and Holborn Hill. Partly obscured by trees in the centre of the picture is the side of the Station Hotel on Salthouse Road. Close by can be seen a long red brick factory with tall chimney stack which is now demolished and the site forms part of Millom School. Fields beyond the far roof tops are now major housing estates, including Festival Road, Huddleston Road and Pannatt Hill. This postcard was sent from Millom in July 1905 to the Schuckhardt's Hotel in Bad-Nauheim, Germany, and shows the wide circulation Millom postcards achieved in the early years of the century.

13. *Market Street, Millom.* This 1908 view shows a family and summer visitors outside a house thought to be in Market Street, Millom. In 1901 Market Street had a surprising range of commercial activity for what is today almost entirely a residential area. There was insurance broker A.M. Breakwell, confectioner Mrs. R. Mason, draper W. Birkett, grocer Thomas Harling, greengrocer Mrs. C. Johnson and Mr. A. Johnson's boot and shoe shop. Market Street also had a cattle auction, The Royal public house and a motor bus depot. The man shown in the doorway, with a clerical collar, may have been Primitive Methodist Minister, Reverend Stanley K. Chesworth, who lived in Market Street in 1906. In 1906 the street was also home to insurance agent Ernest Roberts, dressmaker Mrs. Fanny Weeks and joiner David Mackereth.

14. *Millom Pleasure Grounds.* Millom Pleasure Grounds on St. George's Road has seen major change since this picture was taken around 1925. A tennis court, bowling green and miniature golf course have replaced the grassed area behind the woman shown on the postcard. The lozenge-shaped tank on the right was a relic from the First World War. Similar tanks stood on beaches and parkland throughout Cumbria as souvenirs of the war. The Millom tank is believed to have been broken up for scrap in 1929. Allotments, just behind the tank, have gone to make way for Millom Sorting Office, Registrar's Office, Millom Hospital and Lapstone House residential home.

15. *Millom school group*. This group of 23 Millom youngsters posed for professional photographer Samuel Lamb outside the solid slate and sandstone walls of Lapstone Road School. They are from class seven and the postcard size picture was produced around 1930. Dozens of similar class groups would have been taken of pupils at Millom's schools in the days before camera ownership was commonplace. The picture features: Jean Stranix, Ida Bennett, Denise Pill, Mary Huddleston, Nelie Jackson, Belle Pennaluna, Gwenie Fullard, Margorie Atkinson, Dora Coulson, Connie Fisher, Florence Phillips, Nannie Steele, Hilda Carter, Mary Noisworthy, Evelyn Giles, Margorie Nicholas, Jean Proctor, Amy Metcalf, Dorothy Eaton, Annie Harvey, Lena Leece, Bertha Rowlands and Ida Myers.

16. *Boer War Memorial, 1905*. This postcard from 1905 shows the Millom war memorial built to honour the soldiers killed in South Africa during the Boer War at the turn of the century. The memorial, to what was then considered a major conflict, was to be dwarfed in size twenty years later by the memorial built to commemorate the dead of the Great War from 1914 to 1918. This elaborately-carved Boer War cross stands on an area of grass outside St. George's Church. The building to the right is the old St. George's Vicarage, which is now a residential home. In 1900 men from Millom, Lancaster, Morecambe, Ulverston, Dalton and Hawkshead had formed the First Volunteer Battalion of the King's Own Royal Regiment. The first of them left home on 16th March to support the Second Battalion and travelled to the South African battles from Southampton on the SS Tagus.

9664            UNVEILING MILLOM WAR MEMORIAL.        SANKEYS

17. *Unveiling Millom War Memorial.* Hundreds of men from the Millom district went to France, Belgium and North Africa between 1914 and 1918 to fight in the war which was claimed would end all wars. Dozens were killed in action and many more injured in battles such as Ypres, The Somme, Arras or Gallipoli. This postcard of around 1920 shows the unveiling of the Millom War Memorial featuring St. George and built in Station Approach, opposite the railway station. A huge crowd watched as the town's civic, military and religious leaders prepared to lay the first wreaths in remembrance of those killed in the First World War. Behind can be seen the corner of Wharton's Garage, Cambridge House Hotel and Millom Masonic Hall, where the foundation stone was laid by Colonel F.R.S. Ewell in June 1901.

18. *Millom War Memorial.* In December 1917 celebrations
were held in Millom and Silecroft for the arrival home of First
World War Victoria Cross holder Tom Fletcher Mayson.
Lance-Sergeant Mayson of the 4th Battalion King's Own Regiment won his award for outstanding valour shown at Wieltje,
Belgium, in July 1917. He tackled two machine-gun positions
single-handed and defended an isolated position against enemy
attack until his ammunition ran out. His home village of Silecroft presented him with a gold watch and an illuminated
address. Despite being wounded twice, Lance-Sergeant
Fletcher survived the war and lived into 1958. Many others
were killed and are commemorated by memorials like this at
Millom, shown around 1920, or at Haverigg and Silecroft.

CAMBRIDGE STREET, MILLOM

19. *Cambridge Street, Millom.* Cambridge Street links Holborn Hill to St. George's Road and Horn Hill and since Victorian times had a mix of commercial and residential uses. The tall building on the right of this undated postcard is now Cambridge House Hotel but at the start of the century was the base for solicitors John Thomas and Wilson Butler. In 1938 Wilson Butler was clerk to the nearby magistrates court and Edgar Satterthwaite was his deputy. Other businesses included hairdresser Evelyn Boynes and milliner Lily Castle. Facing Cambridge House is the freemasons hall of Whitwell Lodge Number 1390 whose secretary in 1938 was William Rook. In 1901 the street was home to George Mudge, the music teacher, and William Millar, the school attendance officer.

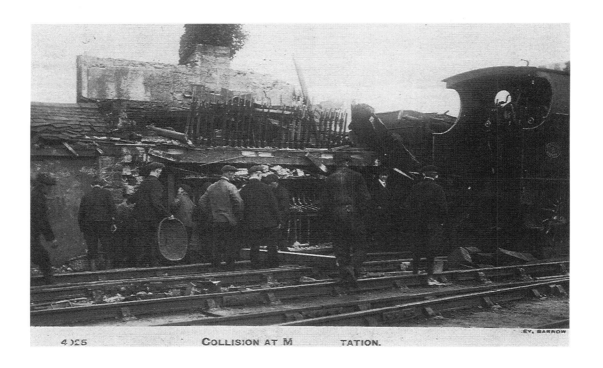

4)25    COLLISION AT M    TATION.    EV. BARROW

20. *Millom Station, collision, 1913*. Millom folk rallied round to help clear the wreckage of a railway collision which blocked the line just north of the town's railway station in 1913. This postcard is part of a set of six produced by Sankey of Barrow and shows what is left of Millom Station's signal box and the tangled remains of an overturned passenger carriage. Also featured is a driver's eye view of the controls on Furness Railway steam locomotive Number 8, shown without its coal tender coupled up. The message on the back of the card refers to another Millom crisis in February 1913, although on a less spectacular scale. It reads: 'There has been a bread famine over the weekend. I was looking for bread last night till past nine o'clock.'

SALTHOUSE ROAD, MILLOM

21. *Salthouse Road, Millom.* Salthouse Road is the main road into Millom from the south and links the open countryside near Millom Castle to the town centre at the railway station. It developed as a superior residential road at the end of the last century and was home to many of Millom's clergy and businessmen. This postcard dated 1927 shows Salthouse Road homes which face Millom School and what was the town's first police station. In 1901 residents included George Mair, the commercial manager at Millom Ironworks, and leading builder William Bradley. By 1938 Salthouse Road was home to Holy Trinity vicar, Reverend Samuel Taylor, Methodist Minister Reverend Robert Trotter, at Wesley Villa, and decorator Fred Bradley.

this is only the front part of the house

22. *Wesley Villa, Millom.* This postcard from 1906 was produced as a Christmas greetings card from Millom's Wesleyan Methodist Minister. The card shows Wesley Villa on Salthouse Road, Millom, the home around that time to Reverend Horatius Hartley. Mr. Hartley and his family are probably those shown standing in the doorway, but the card was posted by a new occupant of Wesley Villa, Lily Alcock. Wesley Villa must have been built just after the turn of the century, as the minister in 1901 was Reverend Josephus Bishop, who lived in Lapstone Road, Millom. In 1938 Reverend Robert Trotter lived at Wesley Villa and by then was responsible not just for the Wesleyan Methodist Church in Queen Street, but also for chapels in Newton Street, Holborn Hill and Haverigg.

23. *Millom School.* Millom's first secondary school, The Institute, opened in January 1905 with just over a hundred pupils and a teaching staff of four led by James Sharp. This postcard by the Raphael Tuck Company shows the Millom Secondary School complex on Salthouse Road. In 1938 the school had places for 180 pupils and was maintained by Cumberland County Council with Mr. H.B. Courchee as headmaster. The buildings shown are now the Upper School of a much larger complex with major additions made in the 1950s. Princess Alexandra opened the new Millom School in November 1959. By that time three hundred pupils attended the school with the new buildings providing places for up to 950.

HOLY TRINITY CHURCH AND MILLOM CASTLE FROM THE KNOT.

24. *Millom from The Knot.* Legend claims that this view of Millom Castle was the same enjoyed by Cromwell's Parliamentarian troops during the English Civil War. Little is known of the siege, in which castle defenders maintaining loyalty to the Royalist cause of King Charles I, faced determined canon fire from the hill side. This picture postcard from the Millom series produced by Illingworth's of Lapstone Road, shows the castle and Holy Trinity Church in 1928. There used to be a Millom Castle School until the Millom School Board made a decision to close it in 1886. At that time the headmaster was Mr. T. Wood. The ring of open countryside around the castle has been steadily eroded by housing developments at Huddleston Road and Pannatt Hill.

On this Spot stood a Gallows the ancient Lords of Millom having exercised Jura Regalia within their Seigniory.

Published by Illingworth. Millom.

25. *Gallows Stone, Millom.* Tucked away in the corner of a field near Millom Castle is a sandstone memorial to the days when justice could be swift and brutal. On this 1902 postcard the wording on the Gallows Stone can be clearly read, but this relic of the once absolute power of the Lords of Millom has been badly worn away by the elements. A 1901 Bulmer's Directory of Cumberland claimed those lords exercised the power of life and death throughout six Millom parishes. 'The Lords of Millom in the days of old must have wielded very considerable influence in the county,' said the directory compilers. The directory said: 'Mr. Thomas Denton, writing in 1688, tells us that the gallows stood on a hill near the castle and that felons had suffered here within the memory of persons then living.'

26. *Millom Road crew.* Transport by railway and coastal shipping allowed the rapid growth of Victorian Millom on open countryside in one of the remotest corners of North West England. Roads in the last century were of greatly variable quality and were used largely for local trips or where the slow speed of horse and cart, or steam powered wagon, or traction engine was acceptable. By the end of the First World War in 1918, petrol-driven cars and diesel wagons were starting to seriously challenge the railways and road improvement and maintenance got a higher priority. This picture of a road crew digging a trench was taken around 1920 by photographer Mr. H. Moore of Hallthwaites, near Millom. The 'Caution, Road Operations' sign in front of them show the crew to be working for the now defunct Bootle Rural District Council.

27. *Millom cheese press.* The making of farmhouse cheeses has been a Lakeland tradition for centuries. This unusual postcard view from about 1910 shows a stone cheese press on a farm near Millom. The picture was taken by Mr. H. Moore, a postcard photographer based at Hallthwaites, near Millom, who specialised in rural scenes. On the back of the card Mr. Moore wrote in pencil: 'A cheese press, 180 years old, on a Cumberland farm. The huge free stone block was lowered by a small piece of wood attached to the wooden crossbeam which squeezed out the whey. Cheeses weighing 40 lbs and over were made with this press.'

28. *Millom reservoir.* The Whicham Valley reservoir shown on this 1911 view played an important role in the growth of Millom. Many of Millom's early terraced streets were built without piped water, but as epidemic diseases became commonplace the town's political leaders were forced to act. In 1875 the Millom Gas and Water Act permitted the borrowing of £10,500 to help provide the town with gas and a regular water supply. Water was a valuable commodity to be argued over by rival local councils. In 1901 Millom industrialist Cedric Vaughan opposed Barrow's plans to use Duddon water by building a reservoir at Seathwaite. As chairman of Millom Urban District Council he claimed a reduced flow of water would silt up the Duddon Estuary and block the outflow of Millom's waste water.

5982       THE HILL, MILLOM.       FROM THE FIELDS BELOW.    SANKEY. BARROW.

29. *The Hill, Millom, 1924.* The Hill of Millom is still a separate and growing settlement, but its closeness to Millom has resulted in the loss of many services. By the 1870s The Hill had a Wesleyan chapel and a chapel of ease to Holy Trinity Church at Millom, built for £575 and with seats for 100. In 1883 a public elementary school was built with spaces for 116 children and by 1901 had 96 pupils in the charge of headteacher Henry Shaw and assistants Miss Petter and Miss Chappell. In 1901 the Hill postmistress was Mrs. Clarissa Anne Foxcroft, Mrs. Jane Rolls was coal agent, Mrs. Sarah Birbeck sold beer from the Miners' Arms and Joseph Dixon Birrell at the Horse Hotel. In 1847 The Hill had three tailors and a shoemaker. This postcard of The Hill was posted by holidaymakers Jim and Blanche in August 1924.

Copyright
T.G. 3.

View from Smithy Hill, The Green

Raphael Tuck & Sons Ltd
London

30. *Smithy Hill, 1905.* The quiet country lane down Smithy Hill into The Green has seen considerable change since this postcard was produced around 1905. Today it is the busy main road from Millom towards Barrow and has been doubled in width. Back in 1905 The Green still had a blacksmith called Moses Jackson Ormandy, who was also an agent for agricultural implements. Other village crafts at the turn of the century included the shoemakers Isaac Clegg and Robert Stable, joiner Thomas Butterfield, miller and grocer Robert Geldart and hoop maker Thomas Thompson. In 1901 Herbert Hewitt was stationmaster at Green Road Station, Anthony Hamilton was the police constable and postmistress was Mary Futer, who was also the village grocer.

THE GREEN
MILLOM

31. *The Punch Bowl inn, 1907.* In the past century the Millom district has lost a good proportion of its public houses and inns. Many country public houses became private homes, as village farm workers became town miners and metal workers. One which has survived is the Punch Bowl at The Green, Millom, which is shown on this 1907 postcard. In 1907 the Punch Bowl was run by Mrs. Margaret Clegg, but its history goes back much further. Back in 1847 the landlord was George Newton, who was described as a victualler, grocer, draper and bacon curer. The Punch Bowl has seen recent extension and alterations and looks set to remain a vital part of village life well into the next century.

THE GREEN INSTITUTE
B & H. MOORE.

32. *Green Institute*. This group of youngsters posing for photographer H. Moore stand outside The Green Institute in about 1912. Bulmer's 1901 Cumberland Directory records: 'At The Green is a public hall erected in 1874 by Mr. Myers of Dunningwell, for the accommodation of the agricultural show, which is held here yearly.' Around the turn of the century the secretary of the Millom and Broughton Agricultural Society was Mr. G.N. Warbrick. In 1881 Mr. H.D. Shardlow was secretary of The Green News Room which is thought to have been based at the institute. The greatly modernised institute is still in regular use as a meeting room and as a base for fund raising events.

Hurdle Jumpers, Green Show, Sep. 1904

33. *Hurdle Jumpers, 1904.* Millom's agricultural community was prepared to put on a show despite the worst the late summer weather could throw at them. But the show could not go on in all circumstances and in 1875 it fell victim to livestock disease. The Ulverston Advertiser of September 1875 reported that the annual show had to be scrapped to prevent the spread of foot and mouth disease among the prize animals, which would have come into close contact on the show field. The report said: 'On account of foot and mouth disease Millom and Broughton Agricultural Society are not holding a show – J.B. Moore, Secretary.' This postcard shows hurdle jumpers at Green Show, Millom, in September 1904.

34. *Quoiting at The Green.* The advent of television and greater mobility through car ownership has seen the decline of many once popular country sports. On this rare postcard of The Green, Millom, around 1904, villagers are seen enjoying a game of quoits. With the Punch Bowl in the background, the group of men and boys watch as circular cast-iron hoops about eight inches across and weighing more than a pound are thrown for accuracy at a stick standing upright on the ground. At the turn of the century The Green also had its own cricket and billiards teams. On the annual Millom and Broughton show day this field was also used for all manner of sports, including hound trails and equestrian events.

35. *Thwaites Mill.* The streams and becks surrounding Millom have been used for centuries to generate power for all means of agricultural and industrial processes. This postcard of around 1905 by H. Moore of Hallthwaites shows the ivy covered Thwaites Mill. The mill would have drawn the power for its mill machinery from the fast flowing water of Black Beck. In 1847 Thwaites Mill was run by corn miller and malster John Blackburne. By 1881 it was in the hands of farmer and miller John Dodgson and in 1901 it had passed to James Singleton.

Hallthwaites

36. *Hallthwaites, 1901.* Today Hallthwaites, near Millom, is a quiet commuter settlement on the fringe of Millom with few of its inhabitants earning a living from the soil. But when this postcard view was taken around 1901 Hallthwaites was a thriving agricultural community with its own group of craftsmen meeting local needs. Hallthwaites was home to the butcher George Shuttleworth and to the woolen mill of J.B. Moore. The mill dated back to at least the 1840s, when James Moore was in charge, and it produced blankets, rugs and carpets. The 1847 Cumberland trade directory listed John Helling as a Hallthwaites joiner and William Hunter as a shoemaker. At that time the Thwaites township, which included Duddon Bridge and Ladyhall, had a rateable value of £1,975 and had 356 inhabitants.

LADY HALL

37. *Lady Hall, 1913*. The historic agricultural community of Lady Hall overlooks the marshes on the edge of the Duddon Estuary. A Cumberland directory of 1881 records the names of prominent Lady Hall farmers Thomas Marr, William Marr and John Sewell. Also recorded as Lady Hall residents were Mrs. Mary Mawson, woodcutter Wilson Allonby, joiner Edward Lamb and Jos Shephard, the water bailiff. Back in 1847 Lady Hall was home to Mr. R. Edmondson, a schoolmaster who probably worked at the nearby Buckman Brow School. This postcard was printed at Hallthwaites and bears a village post office hand stamp from The Green, near Millom, dated 5.30 p.m. on 7th August 1913.

38. *Number one furnace, Millom Ironworks.* Millom Ironworks was a dangerous place to work with its combination of heat, fumes and heavy equipment. The local newspapers of the late 19th century were littered with reports of injuries and fatalities. In May 1875 James Gordon was badly injured falling from the top of a furnace and two months later Mr. W. Clarke, 25, an ironworks' labourer, was drowned in a boiling water conduit. The same year also saw injuries to bricklayer Mr. Jackson, who fell 30 feet from a new furnace, and horse driver John Coward, who was run over by an empty slag wagon. This 1930 photograph shows the number one furnace at Millom Ironworks.

39. *Spray steelmaking, Millom.* The last years at Millom Ironworks were ones of optimism and development which eventually came to nothing. In October 1966 iron flowed for the first time into a new kind of spray steelmaking unit. The Bisra unit converted iron into steel almost instantaneously by high pressure oxygen jets and lime at a rate of 24 tons an hour. It had been developed in Sheffield as a simple, efficient way to produce steel using up to 40 per cent scrap metal. Phase one in the development called for 3,000 tons of spray steel per week by the end of 1968 and 6,000 tons per week in the 1970s. It was never to be as the plant closed in 1968. This photograph from 1930 shows one of the saddle tank steam engines used for hauling wagons on the iron-works rail network.

40. *Years of expansion.* In 1890 the Millom and Askam Hematite Iron Company was formed to join the two Duddon Estuary iron producers. The new company had a capital of £250,000 and could produce up to 350,000 tons of iron a year. Directors of the new company included MP Mr. A.J. Mandella, Thomas Barlow-Massicks, Herbert Campbell, Harry Cook and George Holt. By the end of the First World War it was decided to abandon production at Askam, but the plant was not demolished until around 1938. Millom Ironworks eventually acquired mining or quarrying interests in Barrow, Dalton, Egremont, Middlesbrough and even Spain. This 1930 photograph shows the steel framework under construction for the new Millom Ironworks' sinter plant.

41. *Millom Ironworks' reconstruction.* A report of the March 1937 annual meeting of Millom Ironworks, chaired by Sir Andrew Lewis, described the ongoing reconstruction of the complex. The new number two furnace was said to be in production while number three furnace had been blown out for relining and number one furnace was to be re-constructed. The ore sintering plant had worked throughout the year and a large blower was being installed from the dismantled Askam Ironworks. 'Altogether the works are getting into very good shape,' said a report to the meeting. This photograph of around 1930 shows the newly-completed sinter plant with chimney and dust extractor on the roof.

42. *Sinter Plant, Millom Ironworks.* The 1930s saw a major change at Millom Ironworks, at a time when world trade recession saw many rivals go out of business. In November 1931 Millom Ironworks' general manager was Mr. A. Hibbert, while assistants Mr. H. Stewart Craig were responsible for commercial matters and Mr. E. Tosh for the works. In 1932 three new blast furnaces were built with a capacity of 250 to 270 tons per day and an operating temperature of 1,600 F. A new sinter plant was also installed with a capacity of 600 tons a day and designed to process foreign and Cumbrian iron ores below a half-inch in section. Unlike raw iron ore, the tiny sinter pellets were porous and allowed easy passage for hot gasses in the furnace. This photograph shows ore bunkers inside the new sinter plant.

43. *St. George's Cricket Club*. Life may have been hard for Millom's miners and iron foundry workers but they still found time for sport. This postcard of around 1903 shows the Millom St. George's Cricket Club. The St. George's Cricket Club is just a memory now, but the modern Millom cricket ground in St. George's Road is overlooked by the church spire. Back in 1901 Mr. F. Lawrence was secretary of Millom Cricket Club. By the 1920s the club had risen to prominence in the North Lancashire and District League, with Alec Rigg as captain and Maurice Gill as club professional. Millom still play in the North Lancashire and District League and in 1993 completed an historic fifth successive year as division one champions.

44. *Millom Cup winners.* This undated postcard of around 1910 shows the victorious team in the Millom and district league charity cup. These sportsmen, posing for Millom photographer Samuel Lamb, played soccer, but it was at rugby league that Millom won its greatest successes. Millom Amateur Rugby League Club, now based at Ironworks Road, was founded in 1873 and is accepted as the oldest amateur rugby league club in the world. By the turn of the century Millom had joined the Northern Union and were based at Millom Castle Hotel with Joseph Higgins as secretary. In February 1889 Millom provided twelve players for the Cumberland 15, which played Yorkshire at Hunslet.

45. *Millom Pier, 1903*. This postcard from 1903 has been produced using an amateur picture of one of the steam-powered tugs working from Millom Pier. The ship is probably The Duddon, which helped cargo boats into dock for seventy years, until it was finally scrapped in 1936. Other tugs working from Millom Pier were the Borwick Rails and the Hardback, which was built in 1901. As the pier grew in importance during the late 19th century it had its own staff working for a harbour master. The first harbour master was William Morgan. He was followed by Joseph Holmes and then by Captain James Fairclough of Lapstone Road. Up to 300,000 tons of iron ore per year left Millom Pier by sail or steam-powered shipping and thousands of tons of coal and wooden pit props were brought in.

46. *The Duke at Millom Pier.* On this picture of 1930 The Duke from Glasgow is one of several vessels tied up at Millom Pier for loading or unloading. In a 1901 trade directory it was stated: 'Borwick Rails is a natural harbour or creek navigable for vessels of 200 tons, where iron ore is shipped and coal imported.' By 1960 a Millom Ironworks promotional brochure could claim: 'Vessels up to 1,200 tons cargo, with up to 15 feet draught can be loaded. Direct shipping is undertaken to South Wales and the continent. The port is equipped with robust magnet cranes, and vessels are turned round within 24 hours. A pilot boat equipped with radio-telephone is operated by the company, and ships can be contacted up to 75 miles radius.'

47. *Hodbarrow Mines.* This early photograph from the 1880s or 1890s shows several of the pit heads, engine houses and chimneys of Hodbarrow Mines. Demolition and subsidence since the iron ore mines closed in 1968 has removed nearly all trace of an extensive complex, which employed hundreds of people for a century. In the 1905 Victoria County History of Cumberland details are recorded of the first major ore discovery at Hodbarrow in 1856. It said: 'This deposit yielded excellent ore, and while the company were working it they built workmen's houses on the adjoining Mains without knowing what was beneath them. While sinking a well to supply these houses with water, another large deposit was found.' By 1900 the Hodbarrow Mines had produced almost 13 million tons, which was more than a third of all the iron ore raised in the whole of Cumberland.

48. *Hodbarrow sea wall*. Winning the Hodbarrow iron ore from land both prone to flooding and subsidence on the edge of the Duddon Estuary needed engineering developments on a massive scale. A timber barrier protected the pit workings until 1890 when the stone inner barrier was completed. It was designed by Sir John Coode and allowed the mines to set new production records which saw 540,000 tons of ore raised between March 1892 and 1893. Flooding became a problem again in 1898 when part of the new stone wall subsided. The answer was a second sea wall or outer barrier built from concrete blocks with a clay and furnace slag filling and completed in 1905. This Victorian photograph shows a section of building work underway on a wooden support structure for one of the Hodbarrow sea walls, possibly the outer barrier.

LOW HOUSE FARM, MILLOM

49. *Waterblean Mines, Millom.* This rural scene of around 1915 shows Low House Farm, near Millom Castle. The ivy-covered farm-buildings, with a few modern additions, still stand on the junction of the main A5093 and the Knott Road. Farmland to the right of the picture was once mined for iron ore by the Waterblean Colour and Mining Company. The firm was based at the foot of the Hill, Millom, and produced red oxide and paint. In 1899 its entire stock, including a pair of huge steam engines, was sold by auction. Today the mining area is open grassland used only for farming, leaving little trace of an almost forgotten aspect of iron mining, which was dwarfed in importance by the nearby Hodbarrow Mines.

KIRKSANTON.

50. *Kirksanton.* The success of Hodbarrow Mines sparked a comprehensive search for new reserves of valuable ore on the outskirts of Millom. A total of eight pits were sunk on three acres of land around Limestone Hall at Kirksanton in the last century. The work was done for the Whicham Mining Company, which was formed in 1880 but never found iron in the huge quantities encountered at Hodbarrow. Kirksanton also had the Brockbank Brewery, a corn mill and many centuries ago had a ropewalk for rope making on the village green. This postcard from 1920 shows a general view of Kirksanton village taken from the grounds of Bankfield House.

51. *Silecroft village, 1929.* Around the middle of the last century, before the railway opened West Cumbria to the outside world, Silecroft was an agricultural community quietly meeting its own needs. In 1848 the village is recorded as having just one person who did not live by farming and he was shopkeeper William Johnson. This picture postcard is from 1929, but shows a view of Silecroft which would have changed little from the end of Queen Victoria's reign. Barns and farm houses in the middle of the postcard are still in use today. The narrow route into Silecroft has been replaced by a modern road linking Kirksanton to Valley End Garage, which passes through fields at the front of this picture.

52. *Silecroft Station, 1904.* The arrival of the railway allowed Silecroft to grow and sell its produce in Millom and further afield. Silecroft Station, shown on this 1904 postcard, was built as the next stop to the North of Millom on the Furness Railway. Since 1904 the wooden signal box on the right edge of the postcard has been transferred to the other side of the tracks. Dozens of people in summer outing costumes are shown on the platform waiting for the next train back to Millom after a day at the seaside. Today few passengers use the station and the traditional platform buildings have been demolished and replaced with simple shelters.

6256              BLACK COMBE, SILECROFT.          SANKEY BARROW

53. *Silecroft Brickworks, 1921.* The railway provided rapid transport for heavy industrial products. Silecroft businessmen were quick to take advantage. Iron ore pits were sunk at nearby Kirksanton and attempts to find richer veins of iron in both Kirksanton and Silecroft continued into at least the 1920s. Sand and gravel were also quarried near Silecroft and a brickworks established in the village to make use of abundant local clay. The brickworks kiln and chimney can be seen in the background of this 1921 postcard. In 1881 James Lings was manager of the Silecroft Brick and Tile Works. Many of Millom's Victorian terraces are built with Silecroft bricks.

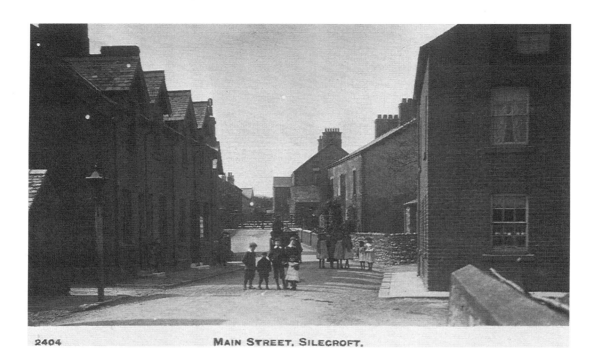

2404  MAIN STREET, SILECROFT.

54. *Main Street, Silecroft, 1916*. By 1880 Silecroft was a thriving village with a wide range of crafts and services. John Henry Bragg was a victualler at the Royal Albert Hotel, Thomas Helme had the Miners' Arms and Thomas Whineray was landlord at the John Bull. The village had two schoolmasters, John Eccleston and F. Matheison, and Thomas Coward who was a barrister at law living at Court End. Thomas Stephens made boots and shoes, Thomas Atkinson was the village joiner and carpenter and William Mason the plasterer. This postcard of 1916 shows Main Street, Silecroft, looking towards the railway crossing gates.

55. *Silecroft post office, 1907.* Silecroft in the 1880s also had its own shops. John Turner was a grocer and draper, John Helme was a shopkeeper and William Knight the postmaster. Stationmaster was Thomas Wilson and William Threlfall was a commercial traveller. This postcard of 1907 shows the village post office run by George Tomlinson. He is seen posing outside the business with his three staff. Mr. Tomlinson was also a grocer, draper and licensed tobacco dealer, selling everything from crockery to Horniman's fine tea. The building shown is now a private house and the village post office and general store has moved 100 yards along the Main Street.

957                        Y.M.C.A. CAMP, SILECROFT                SANKEYS

56. *Holiday Camp, Silecroft.* Fresh air and exercise next to the Irish Sea proved a popular formula for young-sters taking holidays at Silecroft. This fascinating view from around 1930 shows an outdoor fitness class being held at the Young Men's Christian Association camp at Silecroft. Today there is little left to show of all this activity or the extensive chalet complex. In 1943 the Whitehaven News reported that Millom scouts and guides had met Polish scouts and guides who had been staying at the YMCA Camp. It said: 'The visitors always extended a warm welcome to the local scouts and guides, who will retain pleasant memories of the kindness and courtesy of their friends from overseas.'

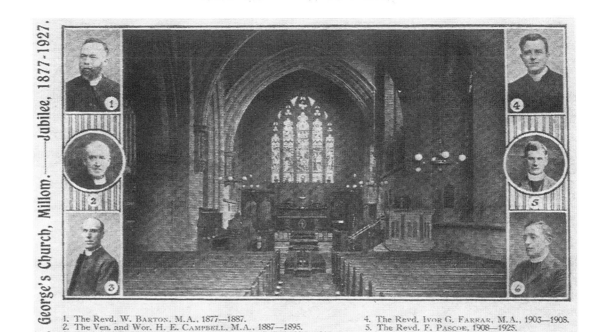

1. The Revd. W. Barton. M.A., 1877—1887.
2. The Ven. and Wor. H. E. Campbell, M.A., 1887—1895.
3. The Right Revd. and Ven. A. E. Joscelyne, D.D., 1895—1903.
4. The Revd. Ivor G. Farrar, M.A., 1903—1908.
5. The Revd. F. Pascoe, 1908—1925.
6. The Revd. H. P. Walton, B.A., 1925.

57. *St. George's Church, Millom.* In 1927 St. George's celebrated fifty years as the parish church of a new town which had changed out of all recognition since 1877. To help celebrate this historic anniversary a series of events was held and souvenirs produced, including special medallions and this commemorative postcard. It shows a view inside the church, looking towards the pulpit, choir stalls and altar. Also shown are the six vicars who served in the parish from 1877 to the golden jubilee year. In 1900 St. George's Vicar, Reverend A.E. Joscelyne, was recorded as earning £300 a year – just under £6 a week. His curate then was Reverend Albert Edward Wyatt. They had to officiate at three Sunday and one Wednesday service, plus Sunday services at St. Luke's Church, Haverigg.

Moss's Series. No. 286.

*St. Luke's Church, Haverigg.*

Millom

58. *St. Luke's Church, Haverigg.* In this 1913 view of Haverigg the village church of St. Luke's stood almost alone in open countryside. Land behind the church has seen considerable development in recent years with the building of several houses and bungalows. Some of the fields are now used for the Butterflowers caravan park and others for pitches and a club house by Millom Rugby Union Club. The house on the left, marked with an 'X', is the St. Luke's parsonage, where the sender of the postcard stayed on holiday. In 1894 the St. Luke's curate was Reverend William Roberts of Sea View, Haverigg, and services at the church were every Sunday at 10.30 a.m. and 6.30 p.m.

59. *St. Luke's Choir, Haverigg.* It has been a long held tradition at Church of England places of worship to have a choir. The choir, dressed in long robes, would lead the singing at Sunday services, even at small village churches. This picture from around 1927 shows the all male choir at St. Luke's Church in Haverigg, near Millom. It shows on the back row W. Smith, J. Singleton, J. Jackson, R. Watters, T. Parrott, J. Woods, J. Mellon, J.T. Martin and J. Martin. The second row shows L. Impson, A. Barrow, H. Hudson, R. Fleming, E. Agnew, J. Cross, T. Floyd, Reverend Doige, Captain Thompson, E. Wilson, S. Wilson and R. Impson. On the front row are J. Troughton, C. Holliday, I. Thompson, H. Woodburn-Park, E. Jeffrey, J. Rogan and T. Holtham.

St. James' Church, Millom.

60. *St. James' Church, Millom.* Shown on this postcard dated 1911 is the interior of St. James' Church in Queen Street, Millom. The church was built in 1888 and in a 1901 trade directory was described as: 'A plain, substantial building, consisting of sanctuary and nave, with two vestries. The east window is of stained glass, circular in form, representing the Holy Trinity.' The cost of building and maintaining the church and nearby school was met by Millom people, many of which worked at Hodbarrow Mines. A surviving mine record signed by 69 miners states: 'We the undersigned do hearby authorize the Hodbarrow Mining Company to deduct fortnightly from our wages the sum of one shilling and threepence each for the Reverend William Perrin commencing July 28th 1883.'

61. *Holy Trinity Vicarage, Millom.* The first vicarage for Holy Trinity Church, Millom, was pulled down for harbouring 'rebels' following the siege of Millom Castle by Parliamentary forces, believed to have taken place in October 1644. In 1781 two cottages near Dashatgate, Millom Above, were converted into a vicarage. This photograph of around 1905 shows the third vicarage, built in 1865 by Canon Irving near Furness Beck, Millom, now called Underwood. The Holy Trinity Vicarage was later in Salthouse Road, Millom, at what is now a guest house. With the joining of Holy Trinity and St. George's into the united benefice of Millom a single vicarage was built on the driveway at St. George's to serve the Churches of St. George's, Holy Trinity, St. Luke's at Haverigg and St. Anne's at Thwaites.

62. *Baptist Church, Millom.* This highly elaborate postcard features the Millom Baptist Church around 1914. The church in Crown Street, Millom, was built in 1884 and was designed to hold a congregation of 280. When this card was produced by Illingworth of Lapstone Road the minister was Reverend A.S. Johnston. In 1906 the minister was Reverend Isaac Lewis, who lived at Finch Villa on Salthouse Road. In 1894 the minister was Reverend Charles Deal from Horn Hill and services were on Sundays at 10 a.m. and 6 p.m. and on Wednesdays at 7.30 p.m. The foundation stone at the Baptist Church was laid by Millom industrialist Thomas Barlow-Massicks in August 1884.

63. *Wesleyan Band, Queen Street.* Music making was a popular pastime in Victorian and Edwardian Millom. The growing town saw the creation of numerous brass bands, orchestras and choirs which played for concerts, competitions and fund raising events. Many have since vanished, including Millom Town Band, but Millom Salvation Army Band and Holborn Hill Royal Brass Band are still playing. This postcard of around 1914 shows a junior band in smart uniforms outside the Wesleyan Methodist Church in Queen Street, Millom. The Wesleyan's held a three-day Japanese bazaar at Millom Co-Operative Hall in 1904 to raise funds for Wesley Villa and entertainment came from Millom Orchestral Band, the Wesleyan Church Choir and the Bible Class Male Voice Choir.

64. *Bible Christian Chapel.* The Bible Christians were one of several non-conformist Christian groups to set up chapels and meeting places in Millom during the last century. Many of the worshippers were former tin miners attracted to Millom by jobs at the Hodbarrow iron ore pits. The Bible Christians had a chapel in Haverigg and the one shown here which has been demolished and used to stand on land in Newton Street, Millom, facing the Cumberland Bus Garage. This group of bandsmen was pictured in 1906 when the Minister was Reverend W.F. Ellis. A Bible Christian sunday school was built to face the chapel in 1894. It has been used over the years as an employment exchange and as a clothing factory.

65. *Salvation Army Fortress*. The Salvation Army Fortress in Nelson Street, Millom, was built in red brick in 1889. It cost £600 and was designed to hold 600 people for services held every weekday at 7 p.m. and on Sundays at 11 a.m. 2.30 p.m. and 6 p.m. Salvation Army founder General Booth made a short visit to Millom in 1905 as part of a county tour and was met by a large crowd in the Market Square. This postcard showing Millom Salvation Army officers, Captain and Mrs. Stein, would have been produced around the time of the visit. In 1983 celebrations were held for the centenary year of the Salvation Army in Millom.

66. *Whicham Church and School.* Whicham Church has nestled under the protection of Black Combe probably since the 12th century, while the nearby school was founded in 1540. The present school room is now a private house, but back in May 1886 the thriving school was given a glowing report in the Ulverston Advertiser. A Whicham Grammar School report had been published following a two-day visit by Mr. J. Sparks, the Queen's Inspector of Schools. He recorded a total of 78 children at the school and said 93 per cent had passed the necessary examination in force at that time. This postcard dated 1909 was issued by W.J. Warnock, who was a Millom stationer.

67. *Whicham Rectory.* A few hundred yards from the school room is the old Whicham Church Rectory. The building at the foot of Black Combe was built in Victoria's reign and is now a private house. It is thought that an earlier Whicham Rectory was burnt to the ground in a raid across the border from Scotland by followers of Robert the Bruce in 1322. A nearby field called Scots Croft is thought to commemorate a battle between Whicham folk and the invading Scots. This postcard by Sankey of Barrow shows the ivy-covered rectory with its own tennis court around 1905.

BEACH VILLA, HAVERIGG.

68. *Beach Villa, Haverigg.* Iron ore mining turned Haverigg from a small fishing community into a bustling village, but the sandy beaches brought a profitable side-line in tourism. Day trippers and holiday makers went to Victorian Haverigg in large numbers. As early as 1880 Mrs. Emma Sage was running The Sea View Refreshment Rooms and the village had three confectioners. Haverigg had no railway station, so horse-drawn 'bus proprietors' sprang up to bring in the summer visitors. This proved a lucrative money spinner for 1880s farmers Thomas Waite of Town End, George Wilson of Hemplings, William Brown of Prospect House and Hannah Mawson of Scale Hook. Shown on this 1914 postcard is a group of visitors enjoying the sand in front of Beach Villa, Haverigg.

Haverigg and Black Combe from the Beach

JV 70098

69. *Haverigg from the beach.* By the mid-1890s Haverigg was a busy village with 2,000 inhabitants relying for jobs mainly on the Hodbarrow Mines. To supply the miners and their families the village developed its own commercial sector of craft skills and traders. Today nearly all commercial activity is restricted to Main Street, but in 1894 there were shops in Caton Street and Sandom Lane and a boot and clog maker in Poolside. The village also had a tinsmith, James Anderson the surgeon, a stone mason, two coal dealers, a painter and a joiner. This postcard of 1914 looks from the Haverigg dunes towards St. Luke's Church and village houses off Main Street.

Main Street, Haverigg

JV 70009

70. *Haverigg post office.* This postcard of Main Street, Haverigg, looking towards Poolside, around 1913, shows what is today the village sub-post office. In Bulmer's 1901 Cumberland Directory the Haverigg village post office was run by Thomas John Corder Fox. He was described as both postmaster and grocer and his Main Street business was given the important sounding title of 'Post, money order and Telegraph office'. At that time the post was delivered each day at 7 a.m. and at 4.45 p.m. Post collections were made at 8.40 a.m, 5.15 p.m. and finally at 7.15 p.m.

645/H2　　　　　　　　　THE BEACH HAVERIGG　　　　　SANKEY

71. *The beach, Haverigg.* This is one of the many postcards of Haverigg produced for the summer tourists to send home as a reminder of their stay. It would have been produced in relatively large numbers and have been on sale in village shops over a number of years until stocks were exhausted. This one is postmarked 1934, but the picture was probably taken around 1920. It shows Concrete Square, Haverigg, which was built in 1872. In 1901 Bulmer's trade directory said: 'Haverigg is fast being transformed from a village into a small town. The Hodbarrow Mining Company have erected a large square of concrete houses, which gives the place quite an air of importance.'

72. *Haverigg Tannery.* Even in 1921 Haverigg retained a wide range of shops and services for a village of its size. Main Street had six shopkeepers, Samuel Mallard, Thomas Evans, Thomas Floyd, William Marshall, Mrs. Troughton and Mrs. Brenda Doidge. Also in business on Main Street was Bennetts and Fred Fox the drapers, James Dawson the joiner, Matthew Newton the butcher, Philip Park, then a fried fish dealer, Sobey Brothers the grocers and hairdresser John Strike. In the late 1920s and 1930s Haverigg suffered very high rates of unemployment due to the effects of a world trade depression. This came at a time of naturally falling employment at Hodbarrow Mines as ore reserves ran out. Shown here is Haverigg Tannery, one of the measures taken to combat the job losses.

HAVERIGG FROM CONCRETE SQUARE.

73. *Pepperhall, Haverigg.* Rows of houses now stand in the place of allotment sheds and chicken runs shown on this postcard by Illingworth's of Millom dated 1921. It shows the view towards Main Street, Haverigg, from the mining community of Concrete Square built by the Hodbarrow Iron Ore Company. The open ground is now Pepperhall and a crescent of homes facing the mouth of the River Lazy and the Duddon Estuary. On the right is Haverigg's Wesleyan Methodist Church, which has been demolished and turned into a car park. It used to have a school room, as well as a chapel with organ, and in the Second World War was the village Civil Defence centre.

Haverigg Duck Hunt.

74. *Haverigg duck hunt.* Hundreds of people line the beach at Haverigg for the curiously named 'duck hunt'. This postcard was never sent through the post, but looks to date from the days before the First World War. It is thought the duck hunt was one of the novelty events staged as part of the Haverigg regatta and water gala held each summer. The main event would have involved serious competition for trophies between sail boats racing around a marked course in the Duddon Estuary. But the regattas also featured swimming, and events on the shore, including stalls and foot races, to keep the crowds entertained.

The Shore. Haverigg

75. *Haverigg Rescue*. In September 1878 there was a daring rescue off Haverigg Point which led to Millom Coroner Mr. Myers-Meakin sending a letter of praise to the secretary of the Humane Society. It said: 'I lay before you the simple facts in relation to a gallant effort to save human life which I venture to say has seldom been surpassed.' A fishing smack with three aboard ran aground in appalling weather and the boat rapidly filled with water. William Thomas, James Willacy and Richard Bond went out in a borrowed boat to find Askam fisherman William Shaw in the water and his brother clinging to the boat mast. A third man from the stricken boat drowned. This 1908 postcard by Illingworth of Millom shows rowing boats on Haverigg beach with fishing craft and Hodbarrow Sea Wall in the background.

76. *Haverigg committee.* This fine group of men in best suits and rossettes are the committee of the Haverigg Workingmen's Club. The club was founded in Victorian days and is still going strong today. It is based at Main Street, Haverigg, with its own patch of allotment land across the road. This postcard view of the club's leading figures would have been taken around 1914. The picture line up shows, on the back row: R. Steele, S. Troughton, H. Holmes, F. Austin, S. Watson, Mr. Gillbanks and Mr. Allday. On the front row: F. Saunders, W. Dawson, F. Fox, J. Metters and E. Bettinson.